DE-CLUTTER YOUR MIND

THE RIGHT MINDSET FOR GETTING THINGS DONE

Copyright © 2018. All Rights Reserved.

No part of this publication may be reproduced, distributed, or transmitted in any form or by any means, including photocopying, recording, or other electronic or mechanical methods, or by any information storage and retrieval system without the prior written permission of the publisher, except in the case of very brief quotations embodied in critical reviews and certain other noncommercial uses permitted by copyright law.

Why You Should Read This Book

Dealing with the inevitable ups and downs of entrepreneurship, goals and life can be challenging, to say the least. So, to help you create the right mindset for success in life, and career. Having the mental and emotional agility necessary for your breakthrough. I have devoted my time, and done tons of research about experts, entrepreneurs, business owners, leaders in many areas of life, advisors. I have reached one conclusion for the right way to be successful in life and everything is simple. Cultivate a wining mindset. It's a can do attitude.

TABLE OF CONTENTS

Why You Should Read This Book... 3 1
Table of Contents.. 4 2
about The Author.. 30 26

Why is it that some people seem to shine in any sphere in which they choose to exert themselves, and others cannot manage even a glimmer despite obvious talent?

Research shows that it's the way that they think about their ability that really counts.

Most of those who have achieved greatness, to use Shakespeare's phrase, have worked extremely hard to get there. Many were told that they would never amount to anything. But they believed that they could achieve, and worked hard to do so.

Developing the right mindset is really crucial to succeed in anything. When a friend of mine was switching his career in 2009 from his co-founded company to a new personal business, he knew that there was a way for him. he kept looking, getting educated, testing, optimizing – and we knew it would pay off eventually. He had a gut-feeling of it. And it did. he was on the right path. He had developed the right mindset.

What is a Mindset?

Your mindset is the sum of your knowledge, including beliefs and thoughts about the world and yourself in it. It is your filter for information you get in and put out. So it determines how you receive and react information.

It's often used for a specific part in your life, as in "the mindset of an entrepreneur" or "the growth mindset". And having the right mindset for what you go for is often the biggest factor.

Developing the right mindset is then the way learning something new and strip out the most relevant information. Then you develop the beliefs that are most helpful for where you want to go or how you want to be. This belief-system is then your mindset.

And I think a good mindset will reflect reality and will help you. But not in that order. I think the order has to be like this:

- Find the beliefs that are most supportive
- Check if the beliefs are in harmony with (a potential) reality

You want to use your mindset to make a positive change. That's why your beliefs don't necessarily have to reflect your current reality. But of course the reality you believe in should be possible. That's like a catch-22, but not really.

If you believe "I am a successful entrepreneur", you will act in that way.

If you believe "I want to be a successful entrepreneur", you will act in this way too: like you are NO successful entrepreneur.

I personally found adopting beliefs that seem slightly out of reach is very powerful. Because it changes your mindset and therefore how you behave. For the better. It let's you grow.

Eighty percent of your capacity to get shit done is in the mind, 20 percent is skill, organization and know-how. So, that's why to get up, get dressed and show up to smashing your success starts with tweaking that mental attitude to taking on the day. The mind is so incredibly powerful and therefore so are you right now.

Why are some people more accomplished than others? Aside from sheer talent, highly successful people have a winning frame of mind that catapults them to untold heights. Billie Jean King had it with tennis. Michael Phelps had it with swimming. Tiger Woods had it with golf. Meryl Streep had it with acting.

Scientists say Mother Nature hardwired us with a negativity bias for survival. The brain is like Velcro for negative experiences and Teflon for positive ones. We routinely assess risks by making judgments about people and situations for safety. To keep us out of harm's way, negative events grab more of our mind's attention than positive ones. You probably remember where you were on 9/11 but not the following week. Forget the blooming azaleas along the roadside. If you don't focus on the car in the other lane zooming ninety miles an hour, you're road kill.

Experts tell us that it takes three positive thoughts to offset one negative thought. No wonder it's difficult to remain hopeful and persevere in uphill challenges where we're bombarded with the same bad-news bias that keeps us safe. We tend to overestimate threats and underestimate possibilities. Without realizing it, we build a negativity lens: the same lousy job, the usual inconsiderate coworkers, or the lackluster party that was nothing to write home about.

From my own personal journey and from studying and working with literally hundreds of leaders globally, I have found some mental exercises key to getting traction in life, work and business. Your success is through developing your mental capacity to smash the glass ceilings that are holding you back and get things done.

Obstacles Stopping You From Getting Things Done

You want to be productive. You want to carpe diem. You want to knock things out of the park.

However, something is stopping you. In fact, there are a few things that are stopping you, but

you can't quite put your finger on what those things are. What's going on?

The good news is that you're not alone. Most people, leaders, startup entrepreneurs experience personal challenges that hold them hostage and impede their progress. These challenges can begin to

shape your mindset about entrepreneurship and their personal success. If you can't get a grip on

what's frustrating you, scaring you or making you lead with trepidation, chances are, your business could suffer, your personal life could suffer.

Re-shaping your mindset about everything takes fortitude and will-power. There will be

days when business looks dim and it'll make you question your capabilities as an entrepreneur.

And of course, there will be really amazing days that seem like you have the Midas touch and

everything works out perfectly. Either way, adjusting and adapting to these moments requires a

mindset that no matter what, you will win.

There are some common traits that leaders and entrepreneurs hold on to that make running a business seem like a battle. The key to becoming victorious over the mindset battle is to know what these traits

are and how to avoid their negative consequences.

Here are few things you need to get over in order get your mindset ready to get things done:

1. Fear

It's not surprising that fear is probably the top thing that's stopping you from getting things done.

From fear of failure to fear of success (yes, it's a real thing), this small but mighty four-letter-

word can turn all of your dreams into a heaping pile of nothingness—if you let it. In order to get

over your fears, you have to face them.

Figure out why you're afraid of moving forward. Could it be finances, opinions of others, bad past experiences, or not enough preparation that's creating a barrier between you and your success? Whatever it is, be honest with yourself about what you're afraid of and come up with a plan to put the fear to rest.

2.The "Right" Time

If you're waiting for your alarm clock to alert you when it's the "right time" to pursue your

Business, or dreams then you're snoozing on your goals. The best solution to finding the

"right time" to make things happen is to just start now.

There'll be some bumps, bruises, setbacks and accomplishments that require you to re-evaluate some things. However, you'll never know what you're capable of until you start doing it. So get started!

3. Money in the Bank

It's always a great idea to have some money stashed away for a rainy day. However, life happens

and sometimes you'll just have to rub two coins together to make things work. There are so

many things you can do while you're saving up towards your business's goals.

You can journal your ideas, do some research, take advantage of free stuff (learning opportunities, software,

contests, networking, etc.) and more. Your goal is to get as much exposure and practice with your ideas that by the time you've reached your monetary goals, you're ready to go full-steam ahead.

And if you're one of those super-risk-taking leaders or entrepreneurs (like myself) who practice

bootstrapping, you can actually get a lot accomplished with a little bit of cash—if you're smart,

strategic and not afraid of the occasional negative balance. Money is a great asset, but it

shouldn't be something that holds you back from getting things done.

4. The Naysayers

Silencing your critics is tough. Everyone has an opinion about what you should or shouldn't be

doing with your business, life or goals. Only trust the advice or information from people with similar

experiences as you.

More importantly than that, trust your gut. The truth is, not everyone in your circle (yep,

that includes family, friends and colleagues) wants you to win. You'll have to develop tough skin

and you'll have to trust yourself a lot more.

Naysayers will encourage you to give up or quit while you're ahead. You could wind up taking their advice—especially if it's from someone close to you. Then you'll never know about your potential or get to soak up the satisfaction of proving them wrong. Learn how to silence the negative chatter and protect your vision or goal.

5. Self-sabotage

Silencing external critics is one thing, but when it comes to silencing your inner critic, that's a

horse of a different color. There will be times when you have an idea, a suggestion or a vision for

doing something and you'll find a way to talk yourself out of it. From negative self-talk like "I

can't do that!" and "Who am I kidding? This is silly.", you can be your own worst enemy.

Do yourself a favor and get out of your own way. Self-sabotage is a surefire way to see your dreams

go up in flames. When you hear yourself sabotaging your success, take a moment to seek

positivity and change the disruptive behavior. Remember, your challenges are meant to make you

better and stronger.

6. Bad Habits

We know that habits are hard to break, but bad habits aren't only difficult, they're detrimental to

your success. Whatever your business bad habits are (unreliability, procrastinating,

over analyzing, being unorganized, etc.), tell yourself that today is quitting day.

Once you recognize the habit, you have two choices: let the habit kick your butt or kick the habit to the curb. You're a smart person. You know what decision that you need to make. Give those bad habits the boot.

7. Not Following Through

You've gotten a great opportunity. You've made it to the next step. You've beat the odds. You can

see the finish line. And now it's your chance to do the final steps and—you do nothing.

Say what?

Poor follow-through skills can cause you to fail every time. It can be linked to fear of

failure or fear of success. It can also be linked to improper training or not wanting to be

victorious.

Either way, if you don't follow through, then you don't reach the finish line and see

what your results are. Ambition is great, but it's nothing without follow-through. So whatever

"open items" you have on the table, see to it that you complete them and check them off of your list. Don't disappoint yourself or anyone else because you didn't finish the job. Get it done.

Incorporate the Winning Mindset

Are you missing the "winning mindset" you need to get things accomplished? Does it seem as if there is an invisible anchor tied to your ambition and creativity you just can't shake? We all have days, or sometimes even weeks, that aren't our most successful or productive. It's inevitable.

But I've got some good tips to help you get back into that winning mindset flow. In no time at all, you will be back to champion status.

Are You Out Of Flow?

You know that you're missing that winning mindset when you are out of flow. But what does out of flow mean exactly? It's a bit of a personal experience, but for most, out of flow moments include the inability to get the tasks done that you need to, your self-talk is critical, you're tired and maybe even crabby, your focus is diluted and your planning skills feel like they've evaporated into thin air.

Now let's compare that to in flow. Your days go by quickly, you feel accomplished in your to-do list, you are having fun, your self-talk is positive and encouraging, you're nice to others and you feel purposeful. Which would you rather be – in or out of flow? Silly question right?

Getting In Flow With A Winning Mindset

Establishing a winning mindset and keeping it isn't as difficult as you might think. Sure, when your runaway brain is in the middle of creating chronic doomsday scenarios, it might feel rather overwhelming. But it definitely doesn't have to be.

Managing Your Runaway Brain

Let's start with the #1 culprit of mayhem, our runaway brain. What's actually going on inside our head has everything to do with what we're feeling. The good news here, is that we can change what we're thinking. And then guess what? Our feelings change. This might sound pretty simple, and it can be, but breaking it down more clearly will help you understand how to build a routine that supports behaviors keeping you in that winning mindset.

Back to the doomsday scenario going on in your head...you know exactly what I mean when I say that, don't pretend that you don't. Its the images of you taking a sales presentation at work that you know like the back of your hand, convincing yourself that your heartburn is a sign of some rare disease you will undoubtedly die from within the next week or worse yet forgetting to pick up your child from school. Generally it's irrational, you recognize it, but you let your brain take you there anyway.

"Establishing a winning mindset and keeping it isn't as difficult as you might think."

How to Change Your Mindset

The following list can help you to develop the right mindset for your situation:

Get the Best Information Only

Try to find the very best information in your field. Then focus on learning this information only. I personally learned that in any worthwhile field there is more information available as needed, especially in the internet. You have to narrow down the information input to the most effective. I personally believe that one of the critical personal skills today is not to find information, but to select the best information and avoid the rest.

The Good: Reading great books/information products and some great blogs. Everything else is a waste of time.

The Bad: Mostly not worth it are forums, getting books/information products without researching the field, 90% of blogs. From my personal experience, those are usually things that support procrastination and information overload. The reason is that only a tiny fraction of the information out there is taking you really forward. You have to develop the skill of identifying this kind of information. We are talking about the right mindset here; part of it is not to get sucked into the mediocre area. You want to align yourself with the best out there.

Role Model the Best People

Similar to #1 look for the best people in your field and try to model what they did right. Adopt their kind of thinking and mindset. Follow them. Of course, keep and only add what you think is right for you. That way you can actually improve and personalize their mindset to fit perfectly for you. It's never copying, it's taking what works for you by getting inspiration and quality input.

Now I realize that you can't look into the minds of the best people in your field. But you can get plenty of information about how they are thinking, their advice, what they did. For instance if you are an entrepreneur or self-employed, here are the people that I role-modeled to a certain degree: Stephen Covey, Steve Jobs, Anthony Robbins, Michael Jordan etc.

Examine Your Current Beliefs

Examine your mindset by looking at your current belief-system. Are these beliefs supporting you? Or are there self limiting beliefs? You have to identify those possible blocks and turn them around. Because whether you know about limiting beliefs or not, they are working in your subconscious mind.

To uncover your beliefs ask yourself the right questions about where you want to go and what is standing in your way right now. The key then is to turn those beliefs around by declaring supportive statements on the same belief. To internalize these new supportive beliefs you can make use of affirmations.

Shape Your Mindset with Vision and Goals

A proactive approach to build your mindset is to clearly see where you want to go. Seeing a vision, images describing your end result clearly in your minds eye, will create a strong pull towards this end result. Then go on and break your vision into goals. It will shape your mindset to become conform with your vision.

Learn and adapt from your own experience and always try to look deeper for the real reasons why you get the results you are getting.

Find Your Voice

One of the most beautiful things is when you find your very own way, something what you could call finding your voice. Stephen Covey wrote a book about that and called it The 8th.

To help you find this, answer these 4 question.

1. What are you good at? That's your mind.

2. What do you love doing? That's your heart.

3. What need can you serve? That's the body.

4. And finally, what is life asking of you? What gives your life meaning and purpose? What do you feel like you should be doing? In short, what is your conscience directing you to do? That is your spirit.

Your voice is what you express 100% authentically, it is the unique thing that you can add to the world, because you are who you are. A great way to success and to develop the success mindset. Looking to find what is really you and being critical about every input you get should be part of your mindset. Stay open and flexible.

Your Brain An Ally

If it all begins and ends with the runaway brain, then how can we use it for good versus a source of frustration and self-destruction? With the right approach and care, your brain can absolutely be your ally. Here's how to make it happen.

What's Going On In There?

Your first step is monitoring your thoughts. But, what you will probably quickly realize, is that your warning sign isn't your thoughts, it's your emotions. Maybe you' re feeling anxious, sad or angry. When this happens ask yourself the following questions:

1. What am I thinking that is making me feel this way?

2. What's the story that I'm telling myself?

3. Is the story true?

4. What meaning am I assigning to the story?

As you work through these questions you will likely find that you're telling yourself a story that is unfounded. Your runaway brain has taken you to places that don't exist, and even if they did exist, you can't manage them from the future – you can only manage from the present.

Assigning meaning to the story is another noted skill of the runaway brain. It goes like this...we feel anxious because our brain has created a story that's not true, we tell ourselves the story over and over again until it feels true, we assign meaning to ourselves and our life about the untrue story, and then we make decisions based on the completely unfounded story. Wow! That's a lot of effort for something that doesn't even exist!

A Better Process – Create A New Story

This is where you have opportunity. Opportunity to create the story that you do want to have in your life. The story that is true, empowering and positive.

Once you know what you don't want, you can decide what you do want. And here is the beginning of calling forth the winning mindset that fits your life vision. Spending time contemplating how things should happen in order for you feel productive and focused is where you want your efforts.

This doesn't have to be a difficult or laborious process. In fact, simply reversing the current story, may be all that you need. Move from failure to success. Easy as that.

Consider going about it in this way:

> Step 1 – Write down the top 3-5 key points of the current story.

> Step 2 – Create your new story by transforming these key points to success by reversing them. Write these out as well.

> Step 3 – Take note of the difference in how you feel (your emotions) when you read the new story. Try reading it out loud for an even more powerful impact.

Here's an example.

The story I've been telling myself is...

- I can't finish all the work that I need to during my workday.

- The tasks are never-ending.

- I've never been able to do this job and I'm not going to be able to do it going forward.

- I'm tired and don't feel well because of everything that I have to do.

- My business is going to fail if I can't get everything done.

Instead my story will be...

- I'm easily able to finish the tasks that are important and matter most to my job.

- I'm well rested, feel healthy and do what's necessary to make this true for myself.

- My business is successful and will continue to be successful.

- I like my job, find joy in helping others and feel grateful that I have the opportunity.

Keep Your Winning Mindset Alive

Once you've redesigned your story and adjusted your emotions, you just need to keep it alive. Again this doesn't need to be a lengthy process, but you do need to commit to it. What's important is that you "keep it alive" in your brain. A couple of easy ways to do this might be...

- Dictate the statements into your phone and play them a few times on your way to work or running errands. The sound of your own voice might be a bit strange at first, but it's very effective.

- Write out the list and place it by your bed. Say the bullet points aloud or silently to yourself upon waking. The affirmations you are making will stick with you throughout the day.

- Write the trigger words for each pointon a post-it note and put it in places you where will see it often, like the bathroom mirror or your computer.

- Type out the statements and use them as a screen saver on your phone or computer.

"This is where you have opportunity. Opportunity to create the story that you do want in your life. The story that is true, empowering and positive."

Focus on the upside of a downside situation.

Every loss contains a gain if you look for it. "I have to pay more taxes this year than ever before" becomes "I made more money this year than I've ever made."

Pinpoint the opportunity contained in the difficulty.

Make it a habit to focus on the good news wrapped around bad news. Ask, "How can I make this situation work to my advantage? Can I find something positive in it? What can I manage or overcome in this instance?"

Develop a growth mindset.

Think of a setback as a lesson to grow from instead of a failure to endure. Ask what you can learn from difficult outcomes or failures and use them as stepping-stones instead of roadblocks.

Broaden your scope.

When threatened, your brain is designed to constrict and target the threat like the zoom lens of a camera. This limits your ability to see the bigger picture. Expand your outlook with a wide-angle lens that steers you beyond doom and gloom to bigger possibilities.

Be chancy.

Take small risks in a new situation instead of predicting negative outcomes before giving them a try. "I won't go to the party because I'm afraid I won't know anyone" becomes "If I go to the party, I might make a new friend."

Avoid blowing a negative situation out of proportion.

Don't let one bad experience rule your whole outlook: "I didn't get the promotion, so I'll never reach my career goals" becomes "I didn't get the promotion, but there are more steps I can take to reach my career goals."

Focus on the solution, not the problem.

You'll feel more empowered to cope with life's curve balls when you step away from the problem and brainstorm a wide range of possibilities.

Practice positive self-talk.

After a big letdown, underscore your triumphs and high-five your "tallcomings" instead of bludgeoning yourself with your "shortcomings." Give yourself a fist pump when you reach a milestone or accomplishment.

Hang out with positive people.

Optimism is contagious. When you surround yourself with optimistic people, positivism rubs off.

Strive to see fresh starts contained in adversity.

Failure is neither personal nor final. Envision letdowns as temporary and know that you can overcome them. Every time you get up and brush yourself off one more time than you fall, you succeed. Perseverance increases the likelihood of propelling you to the top of the leader board.

Conclusion

What is it that makes people successful? There are so many answers to this question, and interestingly, very few of them are untrue. Everyone seems to have a different idea as to what it is that makes a person successful, and we all share the need to become one. At its core, success is a result of numerous factors, the ultimate one being productivity.

Look at the people around you. The most successful people in your life don't have it all figured out, but they seem to manage their time and work-life balance. Procrastination is the silent killer of a person's success, but there is a grand secret behind fighting it and reaching the point of productivity.

That secret path is a productive mindset.

Without a productive mindset, you cannot get to do any of the things people consider essential to become successful. Knowing this, it is time to make some changes in the way you think and act. Apply these tips to get the mindset of highly productive people.

1. Control

What do you imagine when you think about time management? Essentially, effective time management is about introducing higher levels of organization in your life. But, on a much deeper level, time management is control over your actions.

2. Understanding

Changing your locus of control will not work unless you understand the techniques and the logic behind these. Just following tips and applying techniques is simply not enough and is very unlikely to fail you if you do not understand their purpose.

How do you see time management? To really understand its psychology, check out the tree story from Secrets of the Millionaire Mind:

"Imagine a tree. Let's suppose this tree represents the tree of life. On this tree there are fruits. In life, our fruits are called our results…It's the seeds and the roots that create those fruits. It's what's under the ground that creates what's above the ground. It's what's invisible that creates what's visible. So what does that mean? It means that if you want to change the fruits, you will first have to change the roots. If you want to change the visible, you must first change the invisible."

What did you learn? To create the right mindset, you need to look at the problem inside out, not the other way around.

3. Responsibility

The third mindset feature you must possess to be successful is responsibility. You cannot be in control over your life and actions unless you are prepared to take full responsibility for them.

4. Habits

We are proud, but also creatures of habit. Our nature tells us to do the same things continuously, create systems in the form of habits. Instead of trying to get rid of this, why not exploit its power?

When you know what you desire and have the skills to achieve it, make a habit out of it.

5. Acceptance

A successful person has a mindset feature called acceptance. This means that they accept who they are, and work with it.

What are your strengths? What are your weaknesses? The first can get you to reach your goals, while the others can pose a barrier. Your goal is not to change the weaknesses, but work around them and exploit the strengths to do this.

So, start by accepting who you are. Set goals that fit your personality, skills, interests, strengths and purposes. You will never become productive if you base your actions on the circumstances, flaws, moods, or urges.

Disclaimer

The information contained within this Book is strictly for educational purposes. If you wish to apply ideas contained in this Book, you are taking full responsibility for your actions.

The author has made every effort to ensure the accuracy of the information within this book was correct at time of publication. The author does not assume and hereby disclaims any liability to any party for any loss, damage, or disruption caused by errors or omissions, whether such errors or omissions result from accident, negligence, or any other cause. (patent, legal consultion)

ABOUT THE AUTHOR

Tiehu Clarke, author, motivational speaker, and a Certified Life & Relationship Coach. Through her coaching and motivational speeches. She helps women and youth by equipping, empowering them with skills and training. That will help them maximize their God-given potential. Discovering God's purpose for their lives, relationship, and career.

After many years of working. In the field of Mental Health as a Therapist and Substance Abuse Counselor. She has found her next calling, and has now set out to help her tribe of women and youth. Find their WHY, and discovering God's plan and purpose for their lives. Through her individual and group counseling and mentoring classes and sessions.

Tiehu believes helping people is what she is born to do and has a deep desire and passion for God. She believes in the truth of God's word, and is audacious to say that there are no limits and impossibilities. She will tell you that our mind is the greatest enemy. Changing negative dogmas. Is a winning application for achieving and living the ideal life that God created us to live. Her motto is, we are all created for greatness.
Tiehu works with clients through private, group coaching, and mastermind groups.

Tiehu is the author of Declutter your mind, the right way for getting things done and Weight Loss for women over 40.

She holds an M.A. in Christian Counseling, B.A. in Psychology, and is an ordained Chaplain. She lives in Fort Lauderdale, Florida. In her downtime, she enjoys listening to worship songs, meditating, cooking, and traveling.

Do not go yet; One last thing to do

If you enjoyed this book or found it useful I'd be very grateful if you'd post a short review on it. Your support really does make a difference and I read all the reviews personally so I can get your feedback and make this book even better.

Thanks again for your support!

www.ingramcontent.com/pod-product-compliance
Lightning Source LLC
Chambersburg PA
CBHW030557220526
45463CB00007B/3106